MUSIC Party Games

Ready-to-use games

CREATED BY
BRENDA KNOWIS

Editor: Kris Kropff
Cover and book design: Brenda Knowis

Printed in the
United States of America

ISBN: 978-0-89328-441-1

Permission to Reproduce Notice

About this Book . . .

Music Party Games offers a wide variety of fun, exciting and interactive ready-to-use music games for parties or gatherings in the classroom, in the choir room or in the dining room!

Each game is presented in an easy-to-follow format, with a list of materials needed. Reproducible pages and game pieces are included. We have also supplied a few of invitation ideas on the next page. With all the games we have provided, you'll have hours worth of fun for you and your guests!

To add even more fun and interest, have plenty of prizes available for winners (and losers). Offer serious or fun music-themed prizes: sheet music, a dictionary of music terms, inexpensive instruments, or CDs, to name a few.

So put on your game face and let the music games begin!

Games, Instructions and Reproducibles

Your party begins the moment your guests receive their invitation. The invitation provides a wonderful opportunity to give a preview of your party and all the fun and games to be had.

Invitations help generate excitement and a clever invitation lets the recipient know that your party can't be missed! So...be creative and make your own invitation, or use one of the designs we have provided.

Note: Use one of the reproducible designs to the left to create a postcard-style invitation. Just photocopy on cardstock at a local copy center. You can also purchase blank envelopes at a local craft center.

You're Invited to a Party!

Date:

Time:

Place:

R.S.V.P.

1 • Guess Who?

Guests can really get creative with this game and it can be a wonderful ice-breaker to help them get to know each other or just to start interesting conversations. A good time to play this game would be while your guests are gathering. Allow approximately 30 minutes to play.

Materials Needed

- Costume accessories
- Paper and pencils

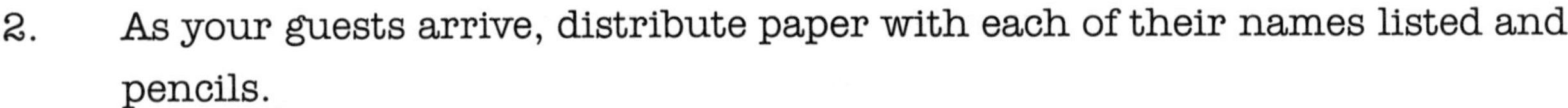

How to play

1. As your guests RSVP to your party, have them select their favorite artist/performer/musician (any era) and find some recognizable costume accessories that they can wear when they arrive at the party. Ask your guests to keep their identity a secret, even from you! Remember…you and your guests can also use items that reflect the artist's personality traits to enhance their costume.

2. As your guests arrive, distribute paper with each of their names listed and pencils.

3. Have your guests mingle in their costumes and encourage them to guess the identities of the other players by asking "yes" or "no" questions.

4. Have your guests write down their guesses next to each person's name.

5. Once all players have had an opportunity to guess, ask each player to reveal the identity of their artist/performer/musician.

6. A point is given for each correct answer and a prize awarded to the player with the most points. Ask all your guests to vote for the player with the most creative costume and present a prize to them, too.

Costume examples:

Madonna - big bow in hair, fish net gloves with fingertips cut off, long necklace with cross

Elton John - big, crazy sunglasses

Ray Charles - dark sunglasses and a big smile

Mozart - white, powdered wig; ruffled collared shirt; overcoat

2 • Composer Cut-ups

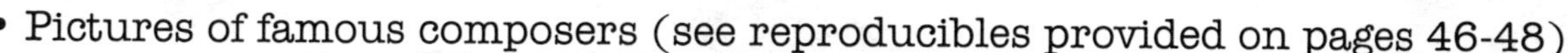

Materials Needed

- Scissors
- Envelopes
- Pictures of famous composers (see reproducibles provided on pages 46-48)

How to play

1. Photocopy the pictures of the famous composers and cut them into horizontal strips where indicated by the dotted lines. (Hairline/forehead, eyes, nose/mouth, chin, neck)

2. Mix up the parts of one portrait and place them in an envelope. Repeat for the remaining composer portraits.

3. Gather the players in a circle. Place the first envelope in the center of the group.

4. Have player #1 draw a strip from the envelope and place it in the center for everyone to see.

5. Ask the players to try to identify the famous composer from the first strip that is revealed by shouting out their answer. If no one is able to guess, play continues.

6. Have player #2 draw another strip from the envelope and place it in position near or next to the first strip. Players should again try to identify the composer by shouting out their answer.

7. Once all the strips have been laid out, the composer's identity is revealed. The first player to shout out the correct answer is the winner.

Answers:

#1 = Schumann	#4 = Brahms
#2 = Copland	#5 = Tchaikovsky
#3 = Mozart	#6 = Beethoven

3 · Common Connection

Materials Needed

- 8 sets of 3 related items
  (see reproducibles on pages 42-45)
- Paper Bags or Envelopes
- Paper and pencils

How to play

1. Photocopy and cut out the *Common Connection* cards on pages 42-45. Each card in the set of three features a picture. All three pictures are connected in some way. Each set is categorized as a person, a song, etc.

2. Place each set of cards in its own paper bag or envelope.

3. Begin playing by opening one of the bags. Remove one card, and hold it up so all players can see it. Have players write down what this item might be connected to. To make the game easier, tell the players the category for each bag of items.

4. Remove a second item from the same bag and show it to the players. Each of the players can make a new guess or keep their first guess. More points are awarded if you are correct on the first guess.

5. Reveal the last item in the bag. Each player can make a third guess or keep a previous guess.

6. Announce the connection between the three items. Players who were right on the first guess get 3 points. Those who were correct on the second try get 2 points; on the 3rd guess, 1 point.

7. Repeat steps 3-6 until all the *Common Connections* have been revealed.

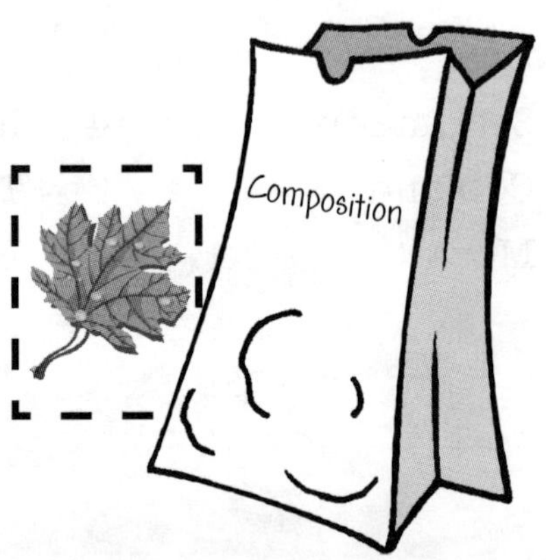

6

4 • Interval Identity • For the serious musician

Materials Needed

- Spinner (see reproducible on page 35)
- Paper clip
- Pencil

How to play

1. Photocopy and cut out the spinner on page 35 and assemble it according to the directions. You may want to mount the spinner to a piece of cardboard for more durability.

2. Have players sit around a table or in a circle on the floor.

3. Choose a player to begin and have that player spin the spinner. Once the spinner has landed on an interval, the player must name a song that begins with that interval. If correct, he or she scores one point and spins again. If the player is incorrect, the next player spins.

4. Play can continue in a clockwise manner and for any length of time you choose. The player with the most points wins.

Examples:

- **Minor 2nd:** "Some Enchanted Evening" from *South Pacific*; Theme from *Jaws*; Für Elise
- **Minor 3rd:** Hey Jude; The Star-Spangled Banner
- **Octave:** Somewhere Over the Rainbow; Let It Snow
- **Major 6th:** Take the A Train; Crazy; To Know Him Is to Love Him
- **Minor 6th:** Laura's Theme; The Entertainer
- **Major 2nd:** Polka Dots and Moonbeams; Happy Birthday
- **Major 3rd:** When the Saints Go Marching In; Swing Low
- **Perfect 4th:** Wedding March; Born Free; At Last
- **Augmented 4th:** "Maria" from *West Side Story*
- **Perfect 5th:** Twinkle, Twinkle, Little Star; Theme from *Star Wars*
- **Minor 7th:** "Somewhere" from *West Side Story*; Theme from *Star Trek*
- **Major 7th:** "Bali ha'i" from *South Pacific* (1st to 3rd note)
- **Unison:** Sleigh Ride; William Tell Overture

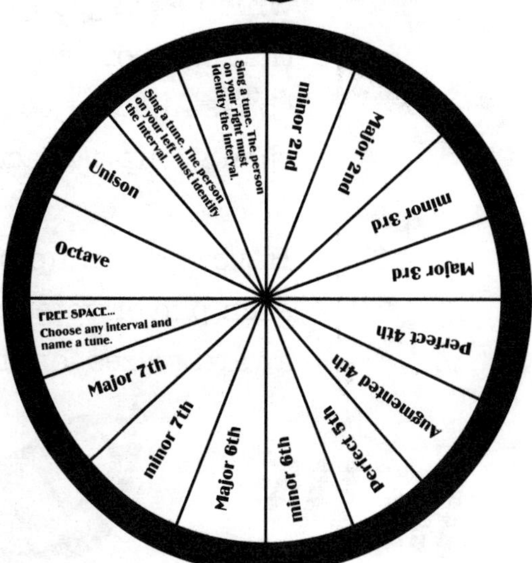

5 • Lots of Laughable Lyrics! • *improv style*

Materials Needed

- Pencils
- Large Pad of Paper and Marker
- *Lyric Sheets* (see reproducibles on pages 36-38)
- *Whacky Words Sheet* (see reproducible on page 39)
- *Music Style Cards* (see reproducible on page 40)

How to play

1. Set out album or CD covers for inspiration. Or, enlarge the album covers at a photocopy center and hang them on the walls to add atmosphere.

2. Choose one of the *Lyric Sheets* and number a large sheet of paper accordingly. Now, select the corresponding *Wacky Word Sheet*. Announce the first category (noun, color, instrument, etc.) and ask players to come up with words that fit the category. You'll need three different words per category. Write the group's words next to the corresponding number on the large sheet of paper.

3. Divide your guests into groups (approximately 4 players in each) and give each group a *Lyric Sheet* and pencil. Have each group use words from the list you just created to fill in their *Lyric Sheets*.

4. Shuffle the *Music Style Cards* and place them face down in a pile.

5. Once all the groups have finished filling in their *Lyric Sheets*, have one player from each group select a *Music Style Card*. This will determine the style in which each group will perform their song, either using a familiar melody in that style or creating their own. To make this easier, you could choose popular songs in advance for each style. Choose artists with a lot of personality that each group can act out along with their performance.

6. Have each group perform their song. Once all groups have had a turn, let each player vote on the group that gave the best performance. You could also award prizes for the worst or funniest performance.

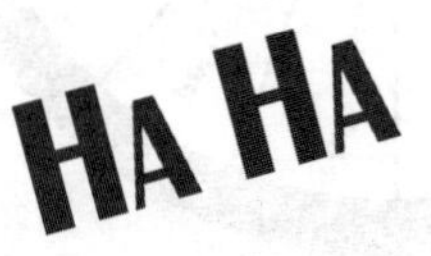

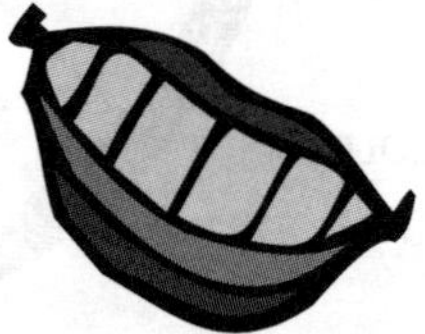

6 • Allegro Alphabet

Materials Needed

• Pencil
• Paper

How to play

1. Choose a guest to be the host of this game. The host will be responsible for awarding points for the players' responses. He or she will need to be quick to write down points next to the player's name as this skit is improvised. Award 1 point for an "okay" response, 5 points for a "good" response, and 10 points for an "exceptional" response.

2. Divide the remainder of your guests into groups of 4 or so and choose one of the groups to go first. Have the host write down each player's name in a column on a piece of paper.

3. Ask the remainder of your guests to participate in each round by yelling out an event related to music, such as "Rock Concert" or "Band Camp." The host can choose the event they prefer.

4. The host chooses a letter of the alphabet. This is the letter that the first player in the group will begin his or her sentence with. For example, if the letter was "S," player #1 might say, "So, how did you like the rock concert?" The next player would have to respond with a sentence that begins with "T," for example, "Totally awesome, man!" Player #3 might say, "Unusual characters, aren't they?" Play continues in this manner until the players have gone through the entire alphabet in succession and are back at "S," the letter you began with. The host is awarding points for each sentence in the conversation.

5. Continue play by choosing a new host and repeating steps #2-4 above with the next group. Continue until all groups have had an opportunity to play a round.

6. Once all groups have participated, tally the scores to determine the ultimate *Allegro Alphabet* winner.

7 • It's in the Clues

Materials Needed

- Paper and pencils

How to play

1. Distribute paper and pencils to everyone and have each player write down the name of a famous musician. They should not show the other players. (You could also play the game with famous compositions, instruments, etc.)

2. Underneath the name, have each player write 5 clues pertaining to the identity of the person he or she chose. Begin with obscure clues and end with more obvious clues.

3. Assign someone to keep score. Have player #1 begin by reading his or her first clue. Anyone who thinks they know the answer may guess. If correct, they get 5 points for guessing correctly on the first clue. Players who guess incorrectly may not guess again. Players who guess the mystery composer on the next clue get 4 points, and so on. Player #1 goes through all clues and reveals the answer before moving on to player #2's mystery composer.

4. The player with the most points wins.

Example:

Mozart

1. I lived from 1756-1791.

2. I composed during the Classical Period.

3. My native country was Austria.

4. I composed 41 symphonies and 21 

5. I was a child prodigy.

8 · The Letter Train

Materials Needed

• Paper and pencils

How to play

1. Write down a music category on a piece of paper so all your guests can read it. For example, you can choose a musical instrument and/or its accessories, song titles, composers, etc.

2. Have players write the letters A to Z down the left-hand side of a sheet of paper. Give your guests 5–10 minutes to write down as many terms as they can that begin with each letter and fit the category chosen.

3. Begin the game by having the players stand in a circle. Have your first player say the name of an item in the chosen category. As an example, say the category chosen is "musical instruments." The second player must give the name of an instrument that begins with the last letter of the instrument given by the first player. The third player must name an instrument that begins with the last letter of player #2's response and so on. Players cannot duplicate another player's answer but may use their "cheat sheets." If a player cannot come up with a response, he or she must sit down. The last player standing is the winner.

Example using instruments:

Player 1:	Clarinet
Player 2:	Trombone
Player 3:	Electric Guitar
Player 4:	Recorder
Player 5:	Reed
Player 6:	Drum
Player 7:	Marimba
Player 8:	Alto Saxophone

Example using music terms:

Player 1:	Alto
Player 2:	Octaves
Player 3:	Scale
Player 4:	Eighth Notes
Player 5:	Slur
Player 6:	Ritardando

Example using musicians:

Player 1:	Ray Charles
Player 2:	(Frank) Sinatra
Player 3:	(Julie) Andrews
Player 4:	Sting
Player 5:	Gershwin

Find the terms listed below in the puzzle and circle them. The words can be straight across, up and down, diagonal, or even backwards. The leftover letters will reveal a fact about Scott Joplin. Can you find the hidden message?

Bassoon	Flute	Percussion	Symphony	Viola
Brass	Horn	Piano	Trombone	Violin
Cello	Oboe	Saxophone	Trumpet	Woodwinds
Clarinet	Orchestra			

```
H  W  O  O  D  W  I  N  D  S  E  W  A
S  P  R  R  O  F  I  C  I  E  S  N  T
P  E  R  C  U  S  S  I  O  N  A  A  T
E  B  O  H  T  Y  H  T  H  B  X  E  B
N  B  T  E  P  M  U  R  T  A  O  N  A
O  J  O  S  A  P  N  D  E  T  P  E  S
B  O  H  T  E  H  O  R  N  P  H  I  S
M  A  N  R  N  O  O  A  I  B  O  N  O
O  C  D  A  W  N  A  S  R  K  N  N  O
R  O  E  W  I  Y  N  A  A  A  E  S  N
T  T  H  L  E  P  S  F  L  U  T  E  K
I  N  G  O  L  S  F  R  C  A  G  T  I
M  E  N  I  L  O  I  V  A  L  O  I  V
```

Hidden Message:

____

____

____

10 · Music Topic Toss

Materials Needed

- *Topic Cards* (see reproducibles on pages 22-23)
- Foam Ball (or create a ball by crumpling sheets of paper)
- Basket, bag or other container
- Watch or clock with second hand

How to play

1. Photocopy and cut out *Topic Cards* (see pages 22-23). Place them in a basket or other container.

2. Ask one player to be judge, timekeeper and scorekeeper. Divide the remaining players into two teams and have each team stand on opposite sides of the room.

3. One player draws a *Topic Card*, reads it and throws the ball to a player on the opposite team. That team has 5 seconds to say a word related to the topic. When Team #1 says a correct word, they throw the ball to Team #2 and that team has 5 seconds to say a word related to the same topic. This continues until a team cannot come up with a word related to the topic, at which point the opposing team scores a point. Teams cannot repeat the other's answer or they forfeit that round. (Some possible "answer" words for each topic are given on page 21.)

4. To continue play, a player draws a new *Topic Card*, reads the new topic, and throws the ball again. This will continue until all topics have been read. The team with the most points wins.

Variation

Instead of answers coming from the entire team, change the rules so that the person who catches the ball is responsible for answering. Let the group decide if a player can answer more than once in a round. If you want to crown an individual winner, each person who can't answer is "out," until only one player remains.

11 • Say It By Ear

Materials Needed

- *Say It By Ear* teasers (see reproducible on page 41)
- Pencils

How to play

1. These little teasers can be great fun for everyone! Each teaser contains several familiar words. When carefully read and sounded out, the words reveal a well-known musician, music term, etc. Prior to your party, make enough copies of the teasers on page 41 for each guest.

2. Have the guests try to solve each teaser. The player who names them first and correctly wins.

Variation: To make this more difficult, write each teaser on a large pad of paper, but mix up the words. Have your guests try to correctly arrange the order of the words to solve the teaser. Your guests should call out their guesses. Have a prize ready for the first player to guess the teaser correctly.

Challenge guests to create their own teasers for your next get together!

"Say It By Ear" Teasers Answers:

1.	Schumann	16.	Allegro con brio
2.	Mozart	17.	*Pictures at an Exhibition*
3.	Meters	18.	Metronome
4.	Mendelssohn	19.	*The Farmer in the Dell*
5.	Bizet	20.	Syncopation
6.	*Für Elise*	21.	Poco
7.	Chopin	22.	Molto
8.	Rachmaninoff	23.	Percussion
9.	Debussy	24.	Saxophone
10.	Beethoven	25.	Duet
11.	Decrescendo	26.	Conductor
12.	*Madame Butterfly*	27.	Classical
13.	Accelerando	28.	Purcell
14.	Diminuendo	29.	Country
15.	*The Sound of Music*	30.	Romantic

12 • Lottery Play

Materials Needed

- *Lottery Play Question Cards* (see reproducible on pages 28-29)
- *Lottery Play Numbers* (see reproducible on page 27)
- Paper and pencils
- 2 Paper bags

How to play

1. Photocopy and cut out the 30 *Lottery Play Question Cards*. Each question corresponds to a different number between 1 and 30.

2. Photocopy and cut out 2 sets of *Lottery Play Numbers*. Put each set (1 through 30) into its own bag and number the bags #1 and #2.

3. Choose someone to be the scorekeeper. Have him or her write the numbers 1 through 30 on a pad of paper.

4. The scorekeeper chooses one player at a time to answer a question. The first player should choose a number between 1 and 30. The scorekeeper asks the player the appropriately numbered question. If the player answers correctly, the scorekeeper crosses out that number on the list and the player is allowed to draw a number from Bag #1. If the player answers incorrectly, the question is placed back in the mix and the player does not draw a number from Bag #1.

5. When all 30 questions have been asked, draw one number from Bag #2. The player with the matching number wins the lottery. You can draw as many winners as you choose and award prizes as you see fit.

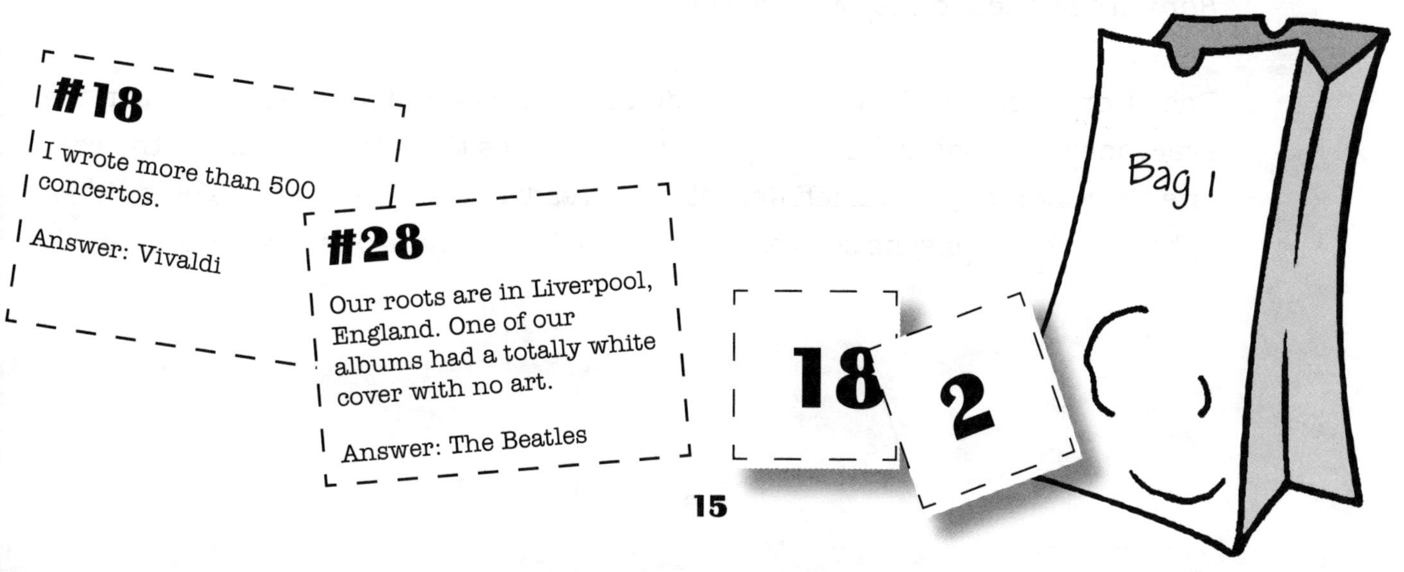

13 • Musical Nonsense

Materials Needed

- *Musical Nonsense Cards* (see reproducibles on pages 33-34)
- Pencils
- *Musical Nonsense Definition Slips* (see reproducible sheet on page 32)

Object

The object of this game is to be the player with the most winning bluffs. That happens by inventing phony definitions for the words on the *Nonsense Cards*. If the other players are bluffed into believing your fake definition is the correct one, you win points. You also win points for identifying the "real" (correct) definition when you hear it.

The main objective is to create definitions that will fool other players. Anything goes. Just use your imagination!

How to play

1. Assign a player to be the "Nonsenser" and lead the first round. (Rotate around the room to select a new "Nonsenser" for each new round.) Hand out *Definition Slips* to all players.

2. The "Nonsenser" chooses a *Nonsense Card*, reads the selected word and spells it out loud. The other players write the word on a *Definition Slip*.

3. The "Nonsenser" copies the correct meaning from the card onto a *Definition Slip*. While the "Nonsenser" is doing this, the other players each invent a meaning for the word that they think will bluff the other players and write it down on their *Definition Slip*. When players are finished, all of the *Definition Slips* are handed to the "Nonsenser."

4. The "Nonsenser" looks over all the definitions, making sure he or she can read everyone's responses. The "Nonsenser" arranges the slips (including the real one) in random order. Each definition is read aloud. After the laughter subsides, the "Nonsenser" may need to read the definitions a second time.

5. Moving clockwise from the "Nonsenser," players guess which definition they think is the correct one. After each player chooses a definition, the "Nonsenser" writes that player's initials on that definition sheet in the "Name" section.

6. After all players have guessed, the "Nonsenser" reveals the true answer and the points are totaled.

7. The player to the left of the "Nonsenser" becomes the new "Nonsenser," and play continues in the same manner.

Scoring: A player earns 1 point for every vote their phony definition receives; a player earns 2 points for choosing the real definition; and the "Nonsenser" earns 3 points if no one chooses the real definition.

14 · Lyric Lingo

Materials Needed

- *Lyric Lingo Cards* (see reproducibles on pages 24-25)
- Paper and pencils, if you chose the variation below

How to play

1. Before game time, photocopy and cut out the *Lyric Lingo Cards* on pages 24-25.

2. At game time, gather players in a circle and explain to them that you will be reading lyrics from familiar songs. The goal is to be the first player to call out the name of the song.

3. Each player who correctly answers first receives a point.

4. Continue reading the song lyrics until they have all been read.

5. Award a prize, such as a CD, to the player with the most points.

Variation

Challenge your guests to create their own lyric samplers. They can score an extra point if they are able to stump the other players!

15 • Alphabet Soup

Materials Needed

- Timer
- Pencils
- *Alphabet Cards* (see reproducible on page 31)
- *Answer Cards* (see reproducible on page 30)

How to play

1. Photocopy and cut out the *Alphabet Cards* and *Answer Cards* from pages 30-31 Once the *Alphabet Cards* have been cut out, shuffle them and place them face down in a pile.

2. Give players *Answer Cards* and pencils. Everyone will have the same categories.

3. Have one player draw five letters from the pile and turn them face up. All players will write the letters down the left-hand side of their *Answer Card*.

4. Set the timer for 2 minutes. The goal is to fill in answers for each category that begin with the selected letters. For example, if the category is "composer" and the letter is "M," the player might write "Mozart." The key to winning is to both be fast and have unique answers.

5. Continue until the time runs out.

6. When time is up, have players read their answers under each category. If any players' items match, they must cross them off.

7. One point is awarded for each remaining answer. The winner is the player with the most points.

Letter	Music Term	Instrument	Composer/Artist	Song Titles	Points
S	Scale	Saxophone	Stravinsky	Some Enchanted Evening	
R	Rest	Recorder	Ravel		
K					

16 • Yes or No

Materials Needed

- Sticky notes or labels
- Marker
- Timer

How to play

1. Before guests arrive, count out one sticky note or label for each player. On each label, write the name of an instrument, musician, music style, etc. When guests arrive, have each player wear a tag on the back of his or her shirt.

2. When game time begins, have all the players sit a circle and choose a player to go first. Have that player stand in the center of the circle and allow the other players to see who or what is written on the tag.

3. Set the timer for 5 minutes and have the first player ask yes or no questions of the group to try and determine who or what is written on the tag. If the player has not been able to guess correctly at the end of the allotted time, no points are awarded. If a player is able to guess on the first question, 10 points are awarded. On the second question, award 8 points. Third question, award 5 points. Fourth question, award 3 points, and anything after that receives 1 point. The player with the most points wins.

Example:

Label = Trombone

First Question: Am I part of the woodwind family? (no)
Second Question: Do I have strings? (no)
Third Question: Am I made of brass? (yes)
Fourth Question: Do I have valves? (no)
Fifth Question: Do I use a slide? (yes)
Sixth Question: Am I a trombone? (yes)

17 • Let's Get Propped!

Materials Needed

- Timer
- Music-related props

How to play

1. Prior to your party, purchase music-related props from a local retailer. For example: toy instruments or instrument parts and accessories (drum sticks, reeds, mouthpiece, strings).

2. Divide your guests into groups of two. Choose two "teams" to be the first to play against each other.

3. Give each team a different prop(s). Set the timer for 1 minute. The goal is to see how many creative ideas each team can come up with to use the prop they were given. Teams can use words to help get the idea across. The two teams should take turns going back and forth with their different ideas.

4. Have your remaining guests vote on which team had the most clever ideas.

5. Play continues with the next two teams and so on until all teams have had an opportunity to participate.

PROP = DRUM STICKS

Music Topic Toss · Topic Answer Examples

Twentieth-Century Composers
- Béla Bartók
- Arnold Schoenberg
- Leonard Bernstein
- Dmitri Shostakovich
- Aaron Copland
- John Cage
- Claude Debussy
- George Gershwin
- Igor Stravinsky

Classical Composers
- Carl Philipp Emanuel Bach
- Ludwig van Beethoven
- Muzio Clementi
- Franz Joseph Haydn
- Wolfgang Amadeus Mozart

Romantic Composers
- Johannes Brahms
- Franz Schubert
- Georges Bizet
- Robert Schumann
- Frédéric Chopin
- Peter Ilyich Tchaikovsky
- Edvard Grieg
- Guiseppe Verdi
- Felix Mendelssohn
- Richard Wagner

Musical Theatre works
- *South Pacific*
- *Hello Dolly*
- *My Fair Lady*
- *The Music Man*
- *Cats*
- *The Producers*
- *Oklahoma*
- *West Side Story*

Pop Artists
- Backstreet Boys
- Britney Spears
- Destiny's Child
- Kelly Clarkson

Jazz Musicians
- Stan Getz
- Miles Davis
- Chick Corea
- Dizzy Gillespie
- Ella Fitzgerald
- Wynton Marsalis
- Charlie Parker

Country Artists
- Shania Twain
- Loretta Lynn
- Johnny Cash
- Tim McGraw
- Hank Williams
- Patsy Cline

Rap Artists
- LL Cool J
- Coolio
- Nelly
- Will Smith
- Jay-Z

Alternative Music Groups
- U2
- Matchbox 20
- Coldplay
- Pearl Jam
- System of a Down
- Chevelle

Rock 'n' Roll Artists
- Elvis Presley
- Chuck Berry
- James Brown
- Everly Brothers
- Jerry Lee Lewis

Classic Rock Artists
- Crosby, Stills and Nash
- Led Zeppelin
- Janis Joplin
- The Rolling Stones
- Aerosmith
- Jimi Hendrix

Blues Artists
- Stevie Ray Vaughn
- B.B. King
- Eric Clapton

Instruments
- Trumpet (Brass)
- Horn (Brass)
- Trombone (Brass)
- Tuba (Brass)
- Flute (Woodwind)
- Oboe (Woodwind)
- Clarinet (Woodwind)
- Bassoon (Woodwind)
- Saxophone (Woodwind)
- Violin (String)
- Viola (String)
- Cello (String)
- Harp (String)
- Guitar (String)
- Piano (Percussion)
- Guiro (Percussion)
- Cymbals (Percussion)
- Conga Drums (Percussion)
- Tambourine (Percussion)
- Timpani (Percussion)
- Xylophone (Percussion)

Musical Styles
- Ballad
- Easy listening
- Pop
- Blues
- Rock
- '60s Rock and Roll
- Jazz
- Funk
- Country
- Rap
- Rhythm & Blues
- Spiritual
- Gospel

Music Topic Toss · Topic Cards

String Instruments	**Facts about Mozart**	**Woodwind Instruments**
Percussion Instruments	**Famous Compositions by Mozart**	**Facts about Beethoven**
Song titles that start with the letter "B"	**Rock - n - Roll Artists**	**Deceased Musicians**
Rap Artists	**Musical Theatre Works**	**Alternative Music Groups**
Pop Artists	**Blues Artists**	**Song titles that start with the letter "M"**

Music Topic Toss · Topic Cards

Song Titles	**Musicians**	**Music Terms**
Instruments	**Country Artists**	**Instruments you would find in an orchestra**
Song titles that start with the letter "S"	**Musical Styles**	**Music Symbols**
Famous Romantic Composers	**Famous Classical Composers**	**Classic Rock Artists**
Famous Twentieth-Century Composers	**Jazz Musicians**	**Famous Compositions by Beethoven**

Lyric Lingo Cards

A country dance was
being held in a garden

Answer:
Polka Dots and Moonbeams

She will promise you more
Than the Garden of Eden
Then she'll carelessly cut you
and laugh while you're
bleeding

Answer:
She's Always A Woman

Harry got up,
dressed all in black
Went down to the station and
he never came back

Answer:
New York Minute

Weather wise,
it's such a lovely day

Answer:
Come Fly With Me

You'll find your fortunes
falling all over the town

Answer:
Pennies from Heaven

The song came and went
like the times that we spent
hiding out from the rain
under the carnival tent

Answer:
Mandolin Rain

Winter, Spring,
Summer or Fall,
All you've got to do is call

Answer:
You've Got A Friend

Why do I feel so spry
Don't wink your eye
Needn't guess, I'll confess
Certain someone just said yes

Answer:
*Looking at the World
Through Rose-Colored
Glasses*

I can hear her heartbeat for
a thousand miles and the
heavens open everytime she
smiles

Answer:
Crazy Love

Butterflies and zebras and
moonbeams and fairy tales,
That's all she ever thinks
about

Answer:
Little Wing

Are the stars out tonight
I don't know if it's cloudy or
bright

Answer:
I Only Have Eyes for You

Walked out this morning
Don't believe what I saw
A hundred billion bottles
Washed up on the shore

Answer:
Message in a Bottle

I resolved to call her up a
thousand times a day and
ask her if she'll marry me in
some old fashioned way

Answer:
*Every Little Thing She
Does Is Magic*

In time, the Rockies may
tumble
Gibralter may crumble
They're only made of clay

Answer:
Our Love Is Here to Stay

And after all this time
I just hope you understand
Sometimes the clothes
Do not make the man

Answer:
Freedom

Lyric Lingo Cards

O the rising of the sun
And the running of the deer
The playing of the merry organ
Sweet singing of the choir

Answer:
The Holly and the Ivy

She'll be wearing red pajamas,
she'll be wearing red pajamas,
she'll be wearing red pajamas
when she comes

Answer:
*She'll Be Coming Around
the Mountain*

I have an ear for music,
And I have an eye for a maid.
I like a pretty girlie,
With each pretty tune that's
played.

Answer:
A Pretty Girl Is Like a Melody

Last night as I lay on my pillow
Last night as I lay on my bed
Last night as I lay on my pillow
I dreamt that my Bonnie was dead

Answer:
My Bonnie Lies Over the Ocean

From glen to glen and down
the mountain side;
The summer's gone, and all
the leaves are falling;
'Tis ye, 'tis ye must go, and I
must bide.

Answer:
Danny Boy

O'er the ramparts we watched
were so gallantly streaming?
And the rocket's red glare, the
bombs bursting in air,

Answer:
The Star-Spangled Banner

Fly's in the buttermilk,
Shoo, fly, shoo,
Fly's in the buttermilk,
Shoo, fly, shoo,

Answer:
Skip to My Lou

The sheep's in the meadow
the cow's in the corn.
But where's the boy
who looks after the sheep?

Answer:
Little Boy Blue

Let martial note in triumph float
And liberty extend its mighty
   hand
A flag appears 'mid thunderous
   cheers,
The banner of the Western land.

Answer:
The Stars and Stripes Forever

In Bethlehem, in Israel,
This blessed Babe was born
And laid within a manger
Upon this blessed morn

Answer:
God Rest Ye Merry, Gentlemen

The one she's been saving,
The one she's been saving,
The one she's been saving
To make a feather bed.

Answer:
Go Tell Aunt Rhody

Leave them alone and they'll
come home,
Bringing their tails behind
them.

Answer:
Little Bo Peep

I told them I was on my way
To old Manhattan Isle;
They all gathered about,
As the vessel pulled out,
And said, with a smile:

Answer:
Give My Regards to Broadway

Mine eyes have seen the glory
Of the coming of the Lord;
He is trampling out the vintage
Where the grapes of wrath are
stor'd;

Answer:
Battle Hymn of the Republic

---

shepherds quake at the sight
Glories stream from heaven
afar, Heav'nly hosts sing
Allelluia

Answer:
Silent Night

Hidden Message Word-Find • It's Instrumental • Solution

Find the terms listed below in the puzzle and circle them. The words can be straight across, up and down, diagonal, or even backwards. The leftover letters will reveal a fact about Scott Joplin. Can you find the hidden message?

Bassoon	Horn	Piano	Trumpet
Brass	Oboe	Saxophone	Viola
Cello	Orchestra	Symphony	Violin
Clarinet	Percussion	Trombone	Woodwinds
Flute			

```
H  W  O  O  D  W  I  N  D  S  E  W  A
S  P  R  R  O  F  I  C  I  E  S  N  T
P  E  R  C  U  S  S  I  O  N  A  A  T
E  B  O  H  T  Y  H  T  H  B  X  E  B
N  B  T  E  P  M  U  R  T  A  O  N  A
O  J  O  S  A  P  N  D  E  T  P  E  S
B  O  H  T  E  H  O  R  N  P  H  I  S
M  A  N  R  N  O  O  A  I  B  O  N  O
O  C  D  A  W  N  A  S  R  K  N  N  O
R  O  E  W  I  Y  N  A  A  A  E  S  N
T  T  H  L  E  P  S  F  L  U  T  E  K
I  N  G  O  L  S  F  R  C  A  G  T  I
M  E  N  I  L  O  I  V  A  L  O  I  V
```

Hidden Message:

He was proficient at both the banjo and the piano and was known as the King of Ragtime.

Lottery Play · Numbers (need 2 copies for the game)

1	2	3	4	5
6	7	8	9	10
11	12	13	14	15
16	17	18	19	20
21	22	23	24	25
26	27	28	29	30

Lottery Play · Question Cards

#1

This style of music influenced early jazz.

Answer: Ragtime

#2

This style of music is often played on fiddle and pedal steel guitar.

Answer: Country

#3

If you see D.C. al Fine, what do you do?

Answer: Go back to the beginning and play until the *fine*

#4

My orchestral work, *Night on Bald Mountain*, was made famous in the U.S. by its appearance in the Disney movie, *Fantasia*.

Answer: Moussorgsky

#5

I was a child prodigy.

Answer: Mozart

#6

I had 20 children

Answer: Bach

#7

A whole note has how many beats in $\frac{4}{4}$?

Answer: 4

#8

What is the term for gradually getting louder?

Answer: *Crescendo*

#9

A timpani belongs to what instrument family?

Answer: Percussion

#10

What is the term for playing with spirit or fire?

Answer: *Con brio*

#11

I died in 1849 at the very young age of 39. I was known for my piano compositions.

Answer: Chopin

#12

I bridged the gap from the Classical Period to the Romantic Period.

Answer: Beethoven

#13

I married Constance Weber in 1782.

Answer: Mozart

#14

I was born in Hamburg on May 7, 1833 and died in Vienna on April 3, 1897.

Answer: Brahms

#15

Mozart said of me, "He will give the world something worth listening to."

Answer: Beethoven

Lottery Play · Question Cards

#16

The music term for playing light and lively.

Answer: *Allegretto*

#17

The music term for accents on the weak beats.

Answer: syncopation

#18

I wrote more than 500 concertos.

Answer: Vivaldi

#19

I composed the magnificient *German Requiem*.

Answer: Brahms

#20

I was known as the "King of Ragtime."

Answer: Scott Joplin

#21

My most famous work was *Messiah*.

Answer: Handel

#22

I am an instrument from the percussion family. I am played by striking mallets on tuned wooden bars that are graduated in length.

Answer: Xylophone or Marimba

#23

Name two composers from the Romantic Period.

Answers include: Brahms, Schubert, Schumann, and Tchaikovsky

#24

Name two composers from the Baroque Period.

Answers include: J.S. Bach, Vivaldi, Handel, and Purcell

#25

Two of my most notable compositions are *The Nutcracker* and *Swan Lake*.

Answer: Tchaikovsky

#26

I was trained by my violinist father.

Answer: Vivaldi

#27

I am part of the string family and Yo-Yo Ma is famous for playing me.

Answer: Cello

#28

Our roots are in Liverpool, England. One of our albums had a totally white cover with no art.

Answer: The Beatles

#29

I was invented by Johann Maelzel in 1816 and I operated on the principle of a double pendulum with a balanced rod weighted at each end.

Answer: Metronome

#30

I am a music style that is heard on Top-40 radio. The songs can be slow or full of driving rhythms.

Answer: Pop Music

Letter	Music Term	Instrument	Composer/Artist	Song Title	Points

Alphabet Soup · Answer Cards

Letter	Music Term	Instrument	Composer/Artist	Song Title	Points

Alphabet Soup · Alphabet Cards

A B C D E

F G H I J

K L M N O

P Q R S T

U V W X Y

Z

Musical Nonsense Definition Slips

Word	
Definition	
Points	Name

Word	
Definition	
Points	Name

Word	
Definition	
Points	Name

Word	
Definition	
Points	Name

Word	
Definition	
Points	Name

Word	
Definition	
Points	Name

Word	
Definition	
Points	Name

Word	
Definition	
Points	Name

Musical Nonsense Cards

Word: balalaika (bah-lah-LEI-kah)

Definition: three-stringed Russian instrument, triangular in shape and similar to a guitar.

Word: raga

Definition: scales used in the music of India which are associated with different moods

---

Word: perdendosi (per-DEN-doh-see)

Definition: dying away

Word: ballabile (bahl-LAH-bee-leh)

Definition: in the style of a dance

Word: idiophone

Definition: an instrument that produces sound by the vibration of the instrument itself

---

Word: pizzicato

Definition: to pluck a string

Word: quodlibet (KWAHD-lih-bet)

Definition: a composition that uses well-known tunes played either successively or simultaneously

---

Word: marcato

Definition: accented, stressed

Word: skiffle

Definition: a British style of popular music of the 1950s, influenced by jazz and blues

---

Word: chaconne (shah-CUNN)

Definition: a continuous set of variations based on a repeating harmonic progression

Musical Nonsense Cards

Word: hemidemisemiquaver

Definition: a sixty-fourth note in England. It is also called quadruple-croche in French, semibiscroma in Italian and semifusa in Spanish.

Word: tremolo

Definition: a rapid alternation of two notes

Word: quindicesima

Definition: 15ma or 15 is the Italian abbreviation for this word and it indicates the interval of a fifteenth.

Word: appoggiaturas

Definition: notes not counted in the rhythm of the measure and are sometimes referred to as "gracenotes"

Word: all' ottava

Definition: means *at the octave* and the abbreviation is *8va* or *8*.

Word: cimbalom
    (CHEEM-bah-lohm)

Definition: a large Hungarian dulcimer

Word: chanterelle (shawn-teh-REL)

Definition: the highest string on a stringed instrument

Word: *sforzando*

Definition: the heaviest of percussive accents and the only one written above or below the note stem

Word: dal segno

Definition: indicates the repeat of extended sections within a composition

Word: zarzuela (tsar-TSWEH-lah)

Definition: a form of Spanish opera where the music is intermingled with spoken dialogue

Interval Identity · Game Spinner

How to use this spinner:

To make the arrow (spinner), unfold a paper clip and place an end over the center of the spinner. Place a pencil on the center point and spin the paper clip.

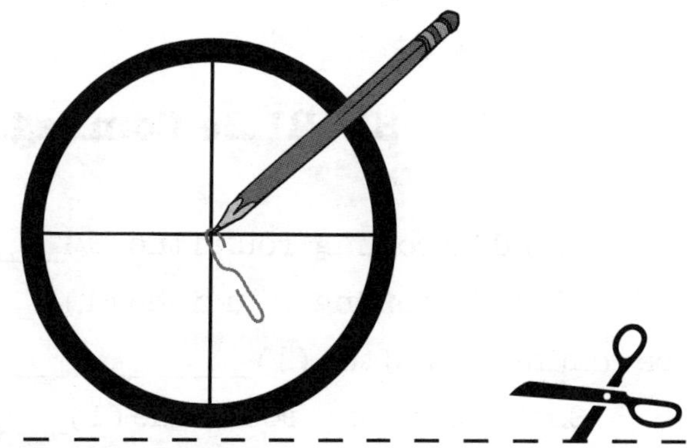

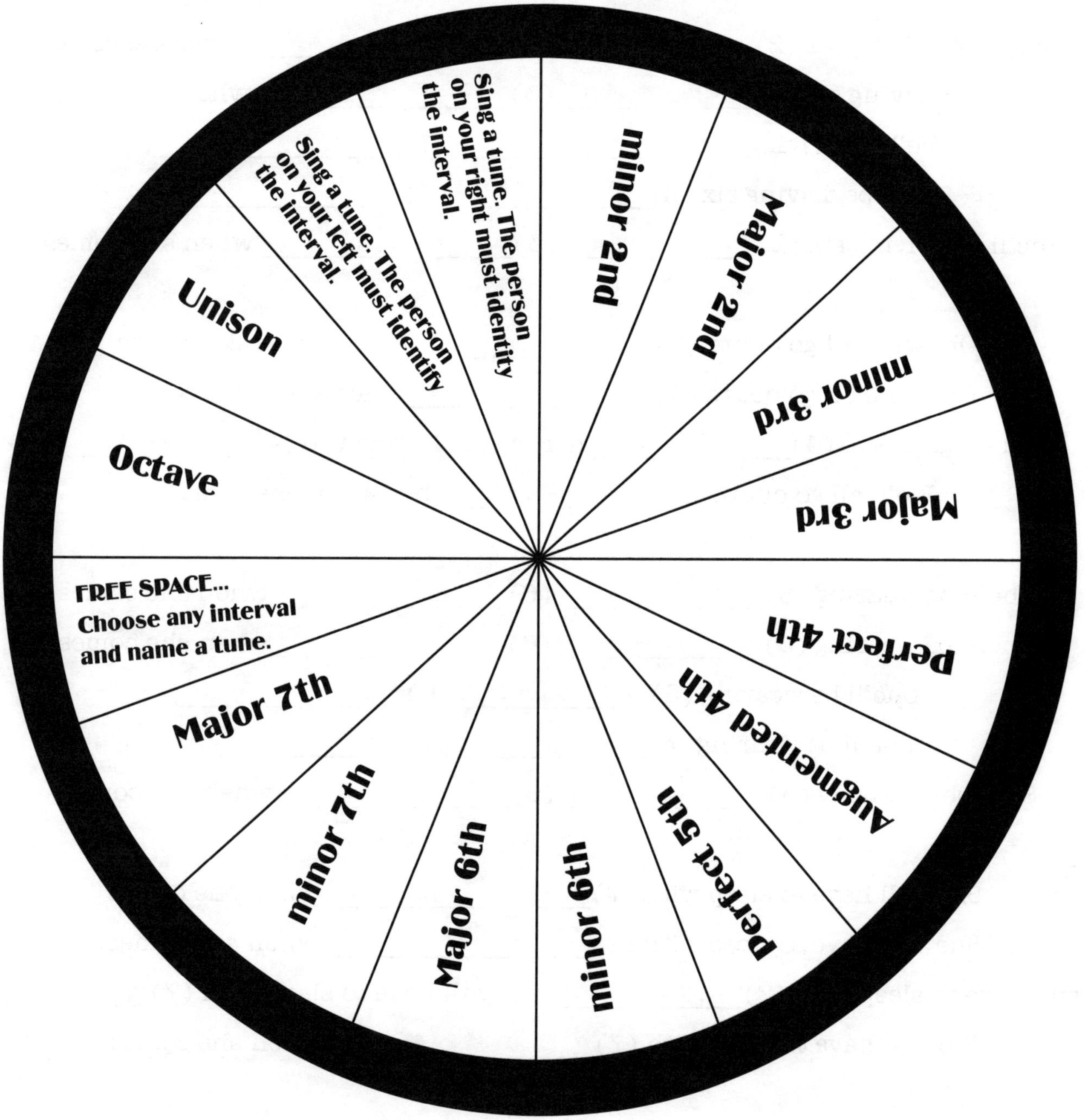

She'll Be Coming Around the Mountain

She'll be coming 'round the (1)_______________________ when she comes

She'll be coming 'round the (1)_______________________ when she comes

She'll be coming 'round the (1)________________, she'll be coming around the (1)______________

She'll be coming 'round the (1)_______________________ when she comes.

She'll be driving six (2)____________ (3)________________ when she comes

She'll be driving six (2)____________ (3)________________ when she comes

She'll be driving six (2)____________ (3)________________,

She'll be driving six (2)____________ (3)________________,

She'll be driving six (2)____________ (3)________________ when she comes.

Oh, we'll all go out to (4)_________________ her when she comes

Oh, we'll all go out to (4)_________________ her when she comes

Oh, we'll all go out to (4)______________ her, we'll all go out to (4)_______________ her,

We'll all go out to _________________ her when she comes.

She'll be wearing (5)_____________ (6)________________when she comes

She'll be wearing (5)_____________ (6)________________when she comes

She'll be wearing (5)_____________ (6)________________,

She'll be wearing (5)____________ (6)______________

She'll be wearing (5)____________ (6)________________when she comes.

She will have to sleep with (7)_________________ when she comes

She will have to sleep with (7)_________________ when she comes

She will have to sleep with (7)______________, she will have to sleep with (7)______________

She will have to sleep with (7)_________________ when she comes.

Lots of Laughable Lyrics! · Lyric Sheet

I've Been Working on the Railroad

I've been workin' on the (1)___________________________,

All the live (2)_______________ (3)________________.

I've been workin' on the (1)___________________________,

Just to pass the (4)________________ away.

Don't you hear the (5)________________ (6)__________________________?

Rise up so early in the morn.

Don't you hear (7)__________________ (8)__________________

"(9)__________________, blow your (10)__________________?"

(9)__________________, won't you blow,

(9)__________________, won't you blow,

(9)__________________, won't you blow your (10)__________________?

(9)__________________, won't you blow,

(9)__________________, won't you blow,

(9)__________________, won't you blow your (10)__________________?

Someone's in the (11)__________________ with (9)__________________.

Someone's in the (11)__________________, I know.

Someone's in the (11)__________________ with (9)__________________.

Strumming on the old (12)__________________.

Fee, fie, fiddle-e-i-o.

Fee, fie, fiddle-e-i-o-o-o-o.

Fee, fie, fiddle-e-i-o.

Strumming on the old (12)__________________.

Lots of Laughable Lyrics! · **Lyric Sheet**

Oh, Susanna

Oh, I come from (1)__________________________

with a (2)__________________ on my knee,

And I'm going to (3)_______________________________

where my (4)____waits for me,

It (5)__________________ all night the day I left,

the (6)______________________________ it was dry,

The (7)_________________________ was so hot, it chilled my (8)___________________,

(9)________________________ don't you cry,

Oh, (9)_____________________,

Oh, don't you (10)______________________ for me,

I come from (1)_______________________

with a (2)____________________ on my knee.

(11)_________________________!

Yankee Doodle

(1)___________________________ went to town, a-riding on a (2)_________________;
Stuck a (3)__________________ in his (4)__________________ and called it (5)________________.

Chorus

(1)_________________________________ keep it up, (1)__________________ dandy,
Mind the (6)________________ and the (7)________________ and with the (8)______________ be handy.

(9)________________ and I went down to (10)______________ along with (11)__________________,
And there we saw the (12)________________ and (13)__________________,
as thick as (14)________________ pudding.

There was Colonel (15)__________________, upon a strapping (16)____________________,
A-giving orders to his (17)___________________, I guess there was a (18)__________________.

Lots of Laughable Lyrics! · Whacky Words Sheet

Oh, Susanna

1. Name of a place
2. Instrument
3. Name of a state
4. Noun
5. Verb (past tense)
6. Noun
7. Noun
8. Body part
9. Person in the room
10. Verb
11. Adjective

She'll Be Coming Around the Mountain

1. Noun
2. Color
3. Animal
4. Verb
5. Color
6. Article of clothing
7. Animal (plural)

Yankee Doodle

1. Name of a person
2. Animal
3. Noun
4. Noun
5. Type of food
6. Noun
7. Noun
8. Noun
9. Proper name
10. Place
11. Person
12. Noun
13. Noun
14. Adjective
15. Proper Name
16. Animal
17. Noun
18. Number

I've Been Working on the Railroad

1. Noun
2. Adjective
3. Noun
4. Noun
5. Noun
6. Verb
7. Person
8. Verb
9. Person in the room
10. Noun
11. Room in house
12. Musical Instrument

Lots of Laughable Lyrics! · Music Style Cards

Jazz	Country	Rap
Rock and Roll	Pop	The Blues
Ragtime	Classical	Classic Rock
Alternative Rock	Hip-hop	Musical Theatre
Funk	Gospel	Ballad

Say It By Ear • teasers

1.   Shoe Man (Clue: Composer) = ______________________

2.   Moats Heart (Clue: Composer) = ______________________

3.   Meat Hers (Clue: Music Term) = ______________________

4.   Men Doll Son (Clue: Composer) = ______________________

5.   Bees Hay (Clue: Composer) = ______________________

6.   Furry Lease (Clue: Famous Composition) = ______________________

7.   Show Pan (Clue: Composer) = ______________________

8.   Rock Man Enough (Clue: Composer) = ______________________

9.   Debut Say (Clue: Composer) = ______________________

10. Bay Toe Van (Clue: Composer) = ______________________

11. Day Cress Send Dough (Clue: Music Term) = ______________________

12. Mad Dam But Turf Lie (Clue: Opera) = ______________________

13. Axe Sell Huron Dough (Clue: Tempo) = ______________________

14. Diamond Ewe End Dough (Clue: Music Term) = ______________________

15. These Hound Dove Muse Sick (Clue: Famous Musical) = ______________________

16. All Egg Grow Cone Brie Oh (Clue: Music Term) = ______________________

17. Pick Sure Sat And Ex Habit Shown (Clue: Famous Composition) =

____

18. Met Row Gnome (Clue: Music Term:) = ______________________

19. Thief Armor Indeed Idle (Clue: Familiar Song) = ______________________

20. Sink Cope Ate Shown (Clue: Music Term) = ______________________

21. Poke Oh (Clue: Music Term) = ______________________

22. Mole Tow (Clue: Music Term) = ______________________

23. Perk Cushion (Clue: Instrument) = ______________________

24. Sack Sew Phone (Clue: Instrument) = ______________________

25. Dew Wet (Clue: Music Term) = ______________________

26. Cone Duck Tour (Clue: Music Term) = ______________________

27. Class Eye Call (Clue: Music Style) = ______________________

28. Purse Cell (Clue: Composer) = ______________________

29. Count Tree (Clue: Music Style) = ______________________

30. Roman Tick (Clue: Music Style) = ______________________

Common Connection · reproducibles

Category: Famous Composition   **Answer:** Stravinsky's *The Firebird*

(Stravinsky)

(Fire)

(Bird)

Category: Music Instrument   **Answer:** Harpsichord

(Harp)

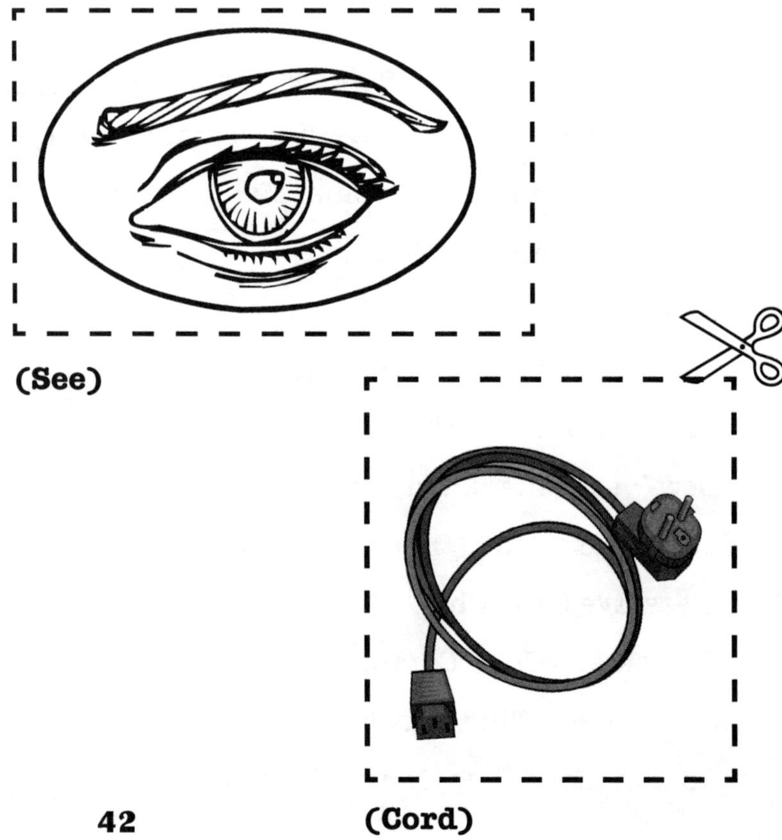

(See)

(Cord)

Common Connection • reproducibles

Category: Famous Composition **Answer:** Mozart's *Magic Flute*

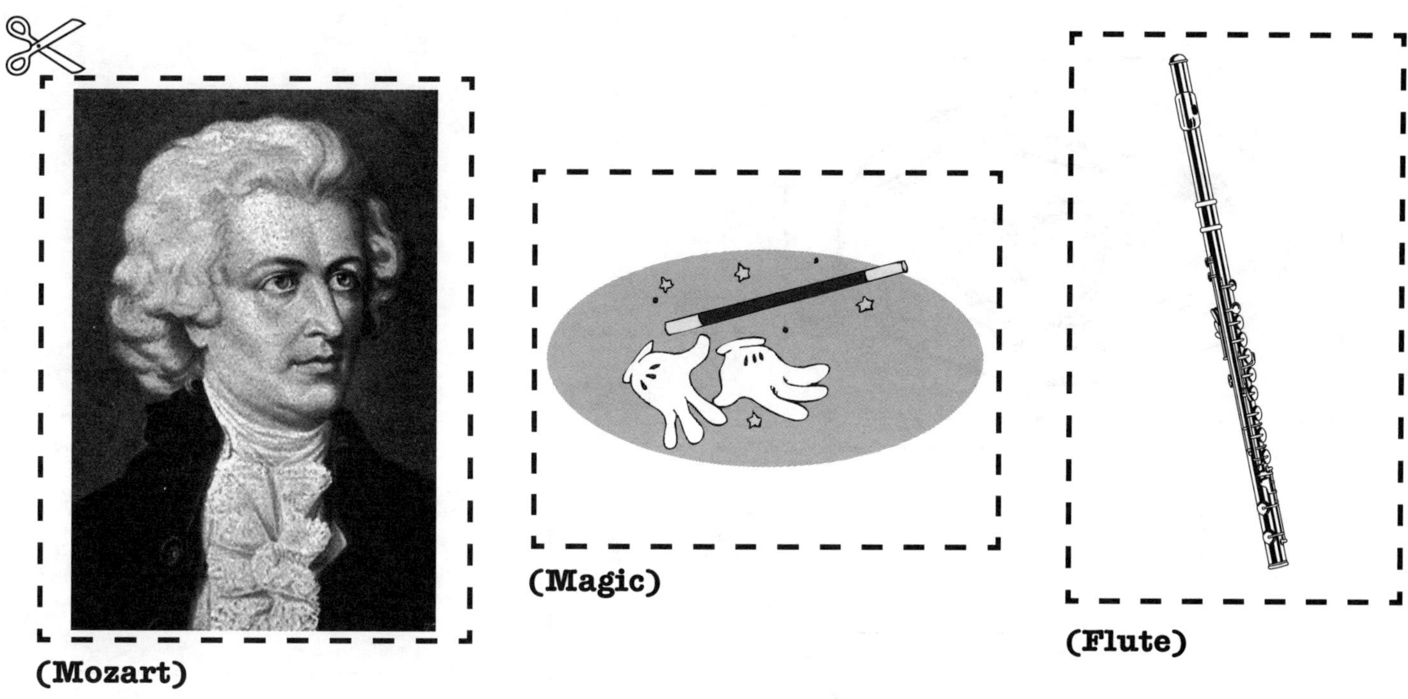

(Mozart)

(Magic)

(Flute)

Category: Music Term **Answer:** Circle of Fifths

(Circle)

5th 5th 5th

5th 5th 5th

5th 5th 5th

(Fifths)

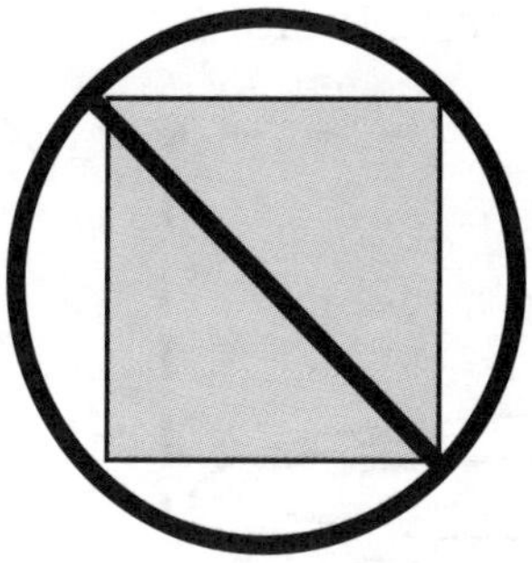

Common Connection · reproducibles

Category: Music Term **Answer:** C Sharp Scale

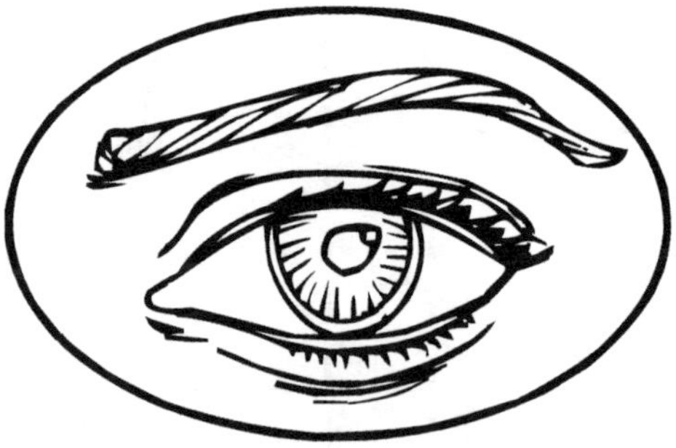

(See)

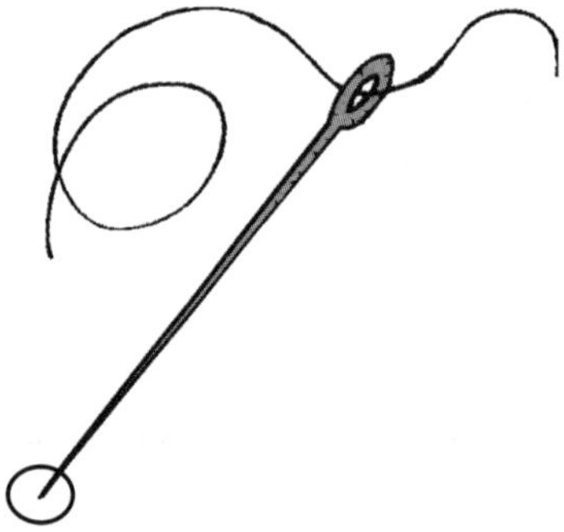

(Sharp)

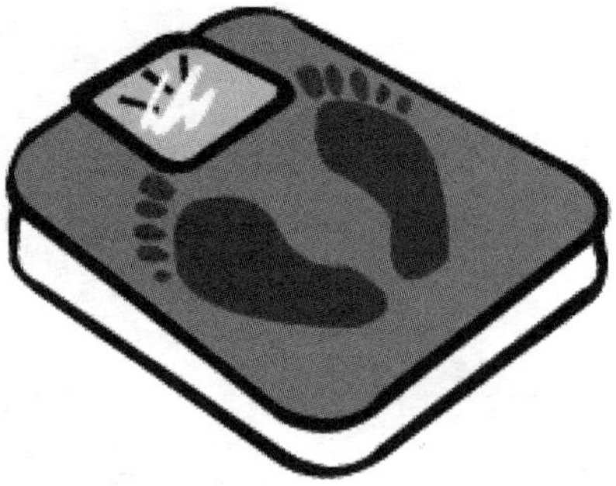

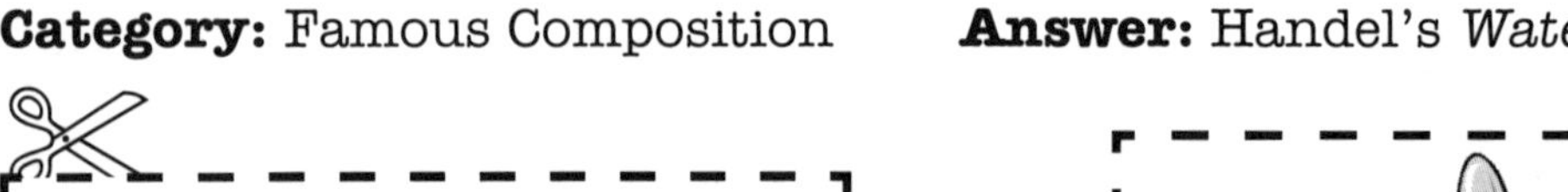

(Scale)

Category: Famous Composition **Answer:** Handel's *Water Music*

(Handel)

(Water)

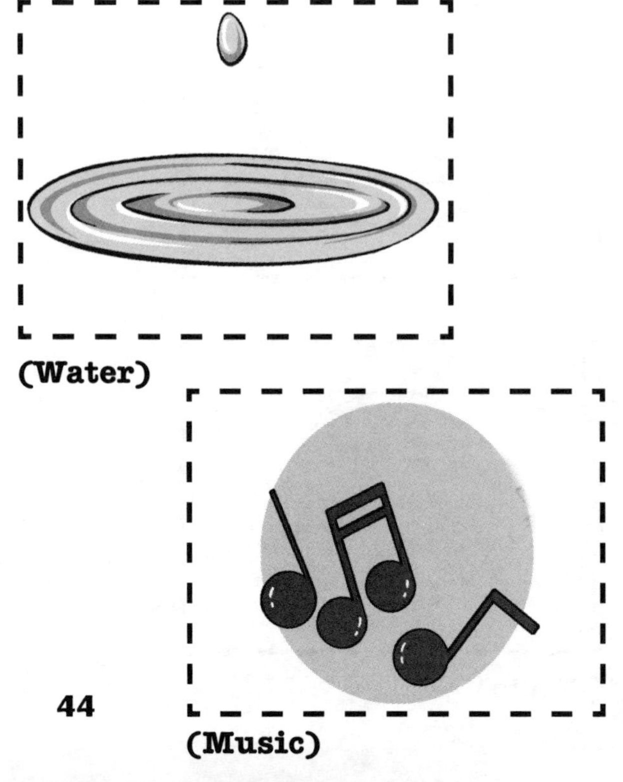

(Music)

Common Connection · reproducibles

Category: Music Style

Answer: Romantic

(Row)

(Man)

(Tick)

Category: Famous Composition

Answer: Joplin's Maple Leaf Rag

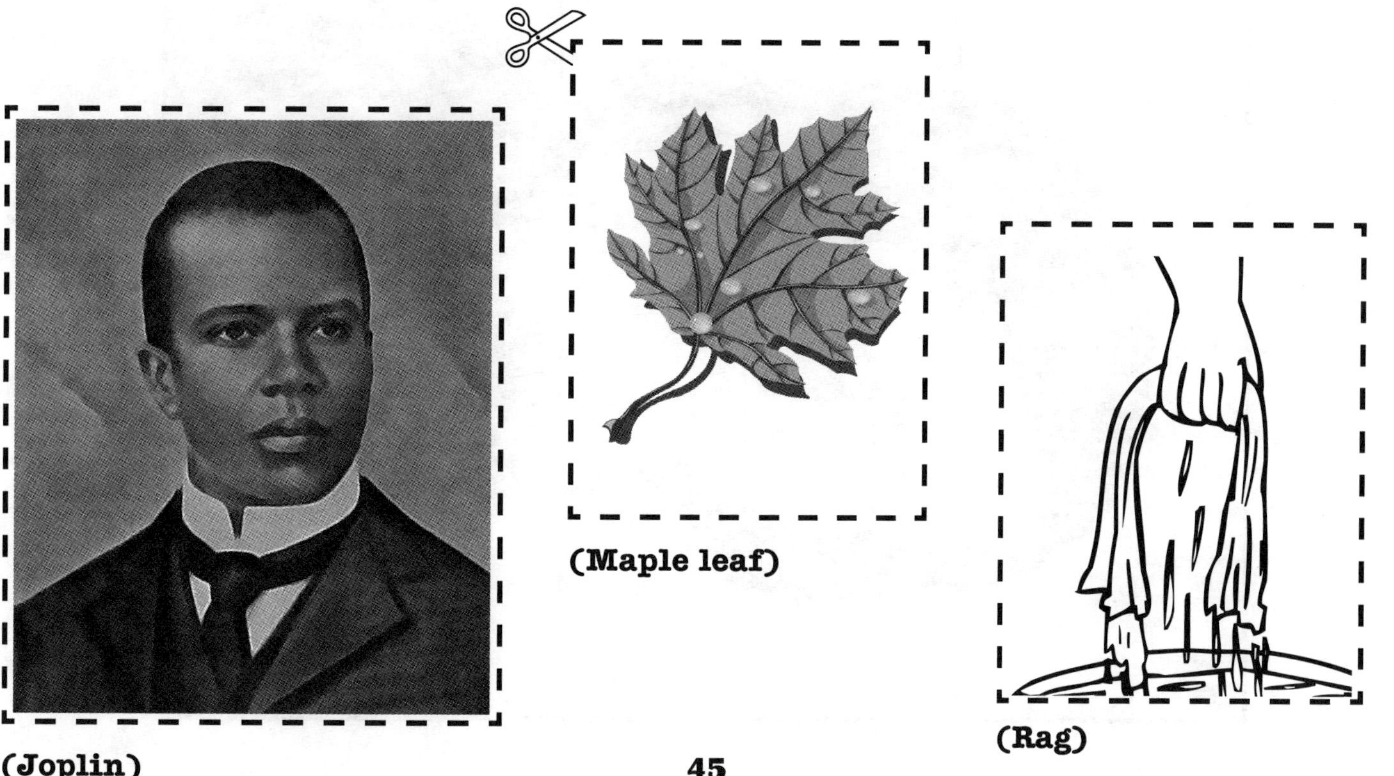

(Joplin)

(Maple leaf)

(Rag)

Composer Cut-ups

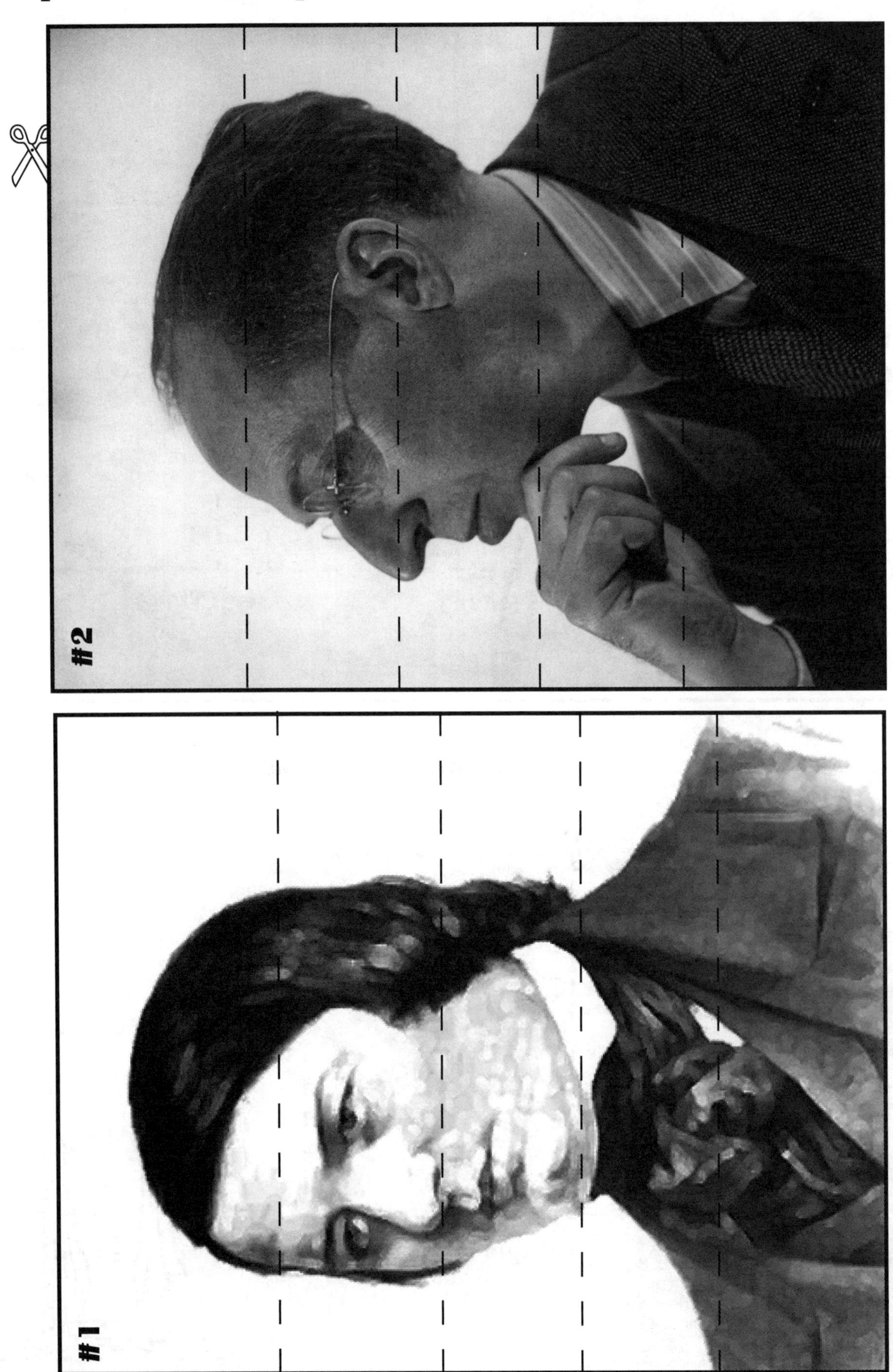

Composer Cut-ups

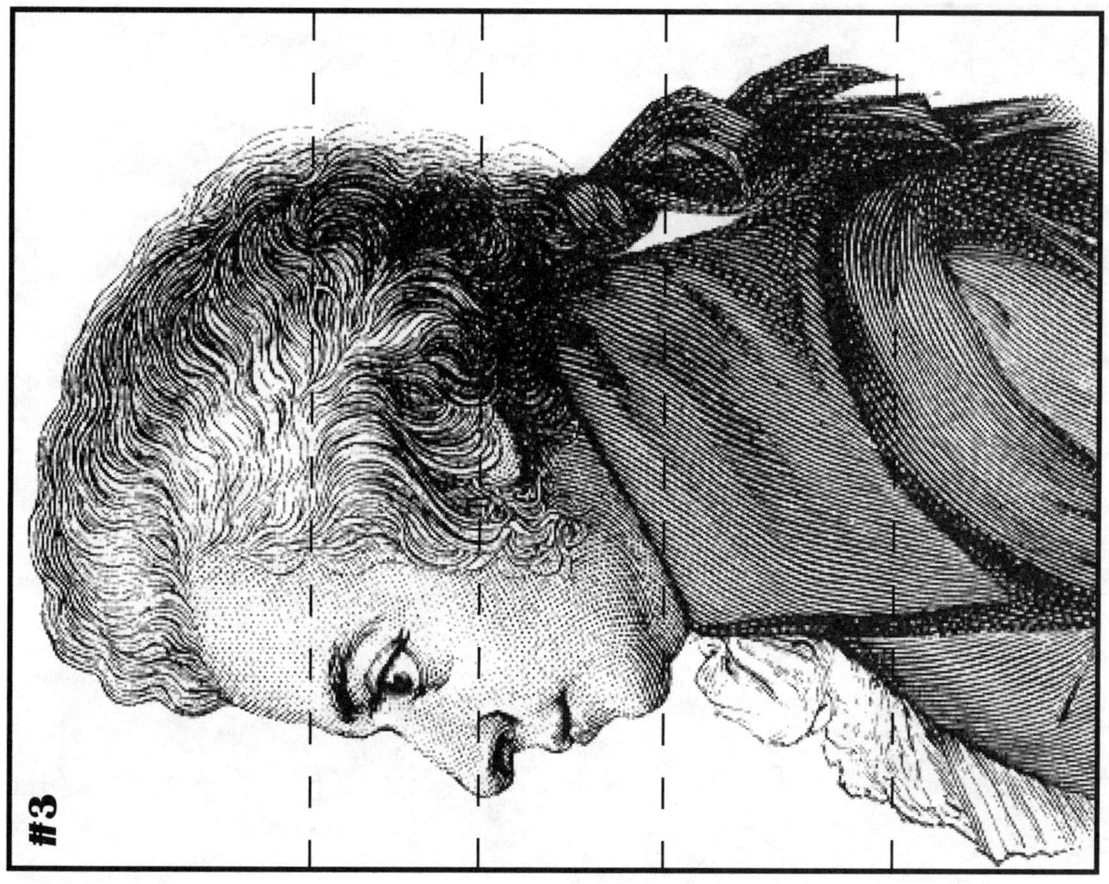

Composer Cut-ups

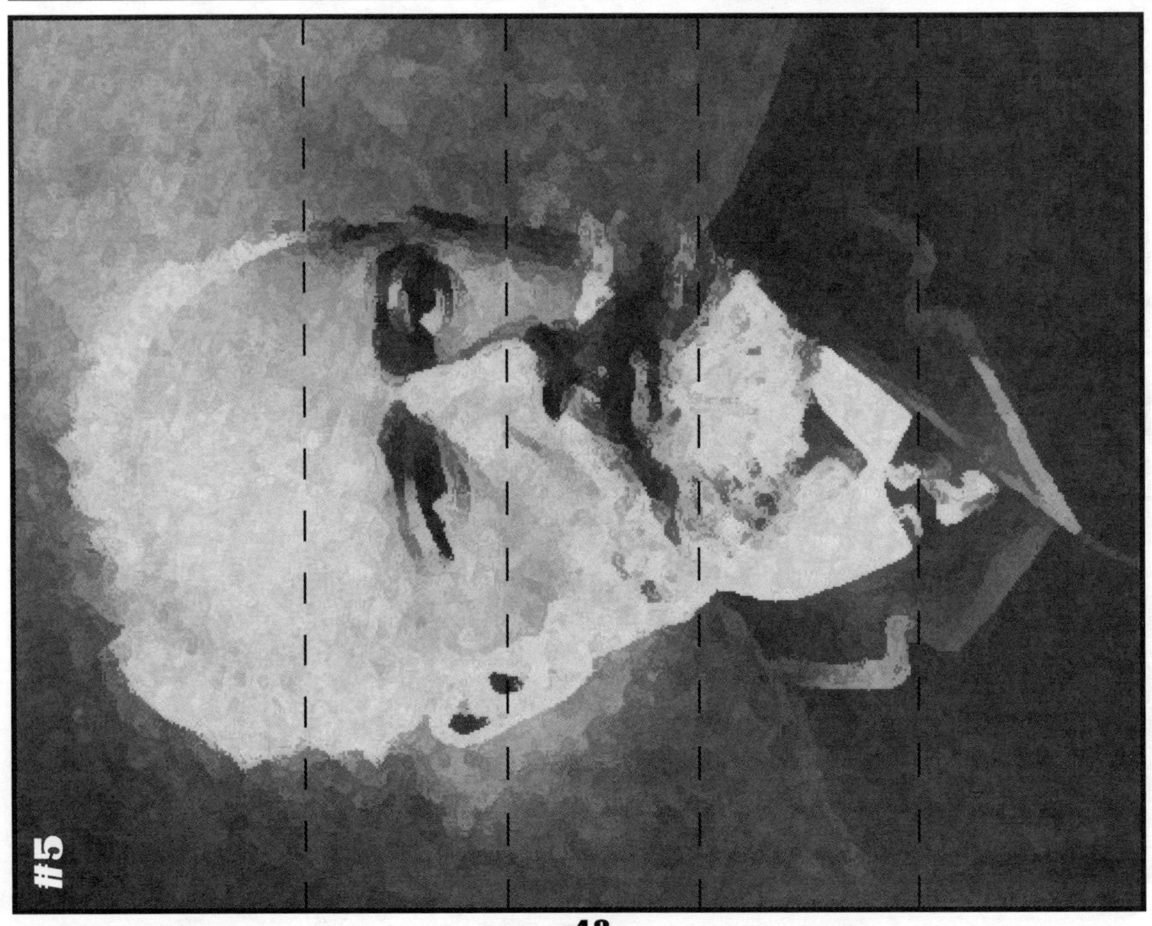